Meg the Shark

By Sally Cowan

Meg the shark swam in the sea.

Meg was very, very BIG!

And she had lots of sharp teeth.

But Meg was sad.

It was hard for her
to make friends!

Other fish swam away from her,
quick smart!

One day, Meg dived down deep,
where it was dark.

She spotted a big squid
with ten long arms!

"My name is Meg," she said.
"Will you be my friend?"

But when Meg gave the squid
a charming smile,
it got a fright!

It darted off and left Meg
in a fog of dark ink.

So, Meg still had no friends.

She did not want to harm others,
but ... she **was** a bit hungry!

She chomped lots of little fish
with her sharp teeth.

When Meg swam up, the stars were out.

A big whale was not far from her.

Meg was not as big as the whale!

"Will **you** be my friend?"
she said.

"No way!" the whale scoffed.
"See this scar on my back?
It's from a shark just like you!"

"It's hard to make friends,"
said Meg.

She looked up at the stars
and felt sad.

Then, a big dark shape jumped up in a big arch.

"I'm Mark the shark,"
he said, with a big smile.

Meg smiled.

Her big sharp teeth looked
just fine to Mark!

CHECKING FOR MEANING

1. How many long arms did the big squid have? *(Literal)*

2. Why didn't the whale want to be friends with Meg? *(Literal)*

3. Why wasn't Mark the shark scared of Meg's sharp teeth? *(Inferential)*

EXTENDING VOCABULARY

harm	What are other words that mean the same as *harm*? What could harm a shark? E.g. people, other sharks, boats.
chomped	What does the word *chomped* mean? How does the –ed on the end of the word change the meaning of the base *chomp*? What other words in the book end in –ed?
scoffed	What does it mean if someone *scoffs*? Why did the whale scoff at Meg? What other words have a similar meaning to *scoff*?

MOVING BEYOND THE TEXT

1. What strategies did Meg use to try to make friends? What else can you do to try to make friends with someone?

2. Describe one of your friends. What do you like about them? Do you have a lot in common?

3. What different kinds of sharks do you know about? Are they all dangerous to people?

4. What can cause harm to our seas and oceans? How can we look after ocean environments?

SPEED SOUNDS

ar	er	ir	ur	or

PRACTICE WORDS

sharp

hard

smart

shark

dark

arms

darted

charming

harm

scar

stars

far

Mark

arch

her